Playing with Plays™
Presents
L. Frank Baum's

THE WONDERFUL WIZARD OF OZ
FOR KIDS
(The melodramatic version!)

For 8-22+ actors, or kids of all ages who want to have fun!
Creatively modified by Brendan P. Kelso
Cover stage illustrated by Shana Hallmeyer
Cover illustrations by Ron Leishman

3 Melodramatic Modifications
for 3 different group sizes:

8-11 actors

10-16 actors

16-22+ actors

Table Of Contents

Foreword .... Pg 4
School, Afterschool, and Summer classes .... Pg 6
Performance Rights .... Pg 6
8-11 Actors .... Pg 8
10-16 Actors .... Pg 38
16-22+ Actors .... Pg 70
Special Thanks .... Pg 104
About the Author .... Pg 105

**To Isidro!
Your continued, relentless support
makes you a wizard in my book!**

-BPK

Playing with Plays™ – The Wonderful Wizard of Oz for Kids

Copyright © 2004-2024 by Brendan P. Kelso. All rights reserved. Used with permission by
Playing with Plays LLC
Some characters on the cover are © Ron Leishman ToonClipart.com. Used with permission.

No part of this book may be reproduced in any form or by any electronic or mechanical means, including photocopying, recording, information storage or retrieval systems now known or to be invented, without permission in writing from the publisher, except by a reviewer, who may quote brief passages in a review, written for inclusion within a periodical. Any members of education institutions wishing to photocopy part or all of the work for classroom use, or publishers who would like to obtain permission to include the work in an anthology, should send their inquiries to the publisher. We monitor the internet for cases of piracy and copyright infringement/violations. We will pursue all cases within the full extent of the law.

CAUTION: Professionals and amateurs are hereby warned that all plays published by Playing With Plays may be produced only pursuant to a signed written license and are subject to payment of a royalty. The plays are fully protected under the copyright laws of the United States, Canada, the United Kingdom, and all other countries of the Berne Union,. All rights, including dramatic (both amateur and professional), motion picture, radio, television, recitation, public reading, internet, and any method of photographic reproduction are strictly reserved.

Whenever a Playing With Plays play is performed, the following must be included on all programs, printing and advertising for the play: © 2004-2023 by Brendan P. Kelso. All rights reserved. Performed under license from, Playing with Plays LLC,
www.PlayingWithPlays.com.

For performance rights please see page 6 of this book or contact:

contact@PlayingWithPlays.com

-Please note, for certain circumstances, we do waive copyright and performance fees.
Rules subject to change

www.PlayingWithPlays.com

Printed in the United States of America
Published by Playing With Plays LLC

ISBN: 978-1-954571-25-9

Foreword

When I was in high school there was something about Shakespeare that appealed to me. Not that I understood it mind you, but there were clear scenes and images that always stood out in my mind. Romeo & Juliet, "Romeo, Romeo; wherefore art thou Romeo?"; Julius Caesar, "Et tu Brute"; Macbeth, "Double, Double, toil and trouble"; Hamlet, "to be or not to be"; A Midsummer Night's Dream, all I remember about this was a wickedly cool fairy and something about a guy turning into a donkey that I thought was pretty funny. It was not until I started analyzing Shakespeare's plays as an actor that I realized one very important thing, I still didn't understand them. Seriously though, it's tough enough for adults, let alone kids. Then it hit me, why don't I make a version that kids could perform, but make it easy for them to understand with a splash of Shakespeare lingo mixed in? And voila! A melodramatic masterpiece was created! They are intended to be melodramatically fun!

THE PLAYS: There are 3 plays within this book, for three different group sizes. The reason: to allow educators or parents to get the story across to their children regardless of the size of their group. As you read through the plays, there are several lines that are highlighted. These are actual lines from the original book. I am a little more particular about the kids saying these lines verbatim. But the rest, well... have fun!

The entire purpose of this book is to instill the love of a classic story, as well as drama, into the kids.

And when you have children who have a passion for something, they will start to teach themselves, with or without school.

These plays are intended for pure fun. Please DO NOT have the kids learn these lines verbatim, that would be a complete waste of creativity. But do have them basically know their lines and improvise wherever they want as long as it pertains to telling the story. Because that is the goal of an actor: to tell the story. In A Midsummer Night's Dream, I once had a student playing Quince question me about one of her lines, "but in the actual story, didn't the Mechanicals state that 'they would hang us'?" I thought for a second and realized that she had read the story with her mom, and she was right. So I let her add the line she wanted and it added that much more fun, it made the play theirs. I have had kids throw water on the audience, run around the audience, sit in the audience, lose their pumpkin pants (size 30 around a size 15 doesn't work very well, but makes for some great humor!) and most importantly, die all over the stage. The kids love it.

One last note: if you want some educational resources, loved our plays, want to tell the world how much your kids loved performing Shakespeare, want to insult someone with our Shakespeare Insult Generator, or are just a fan of Shakespeare, then hop on our website and have fun:

PlayingWithPlays.com

With these notes, I'll see you on the stage, have fun, and break a leg!

SCHOOL, AFTERSCHOOL, and SUMMER classes

I've been teaching these plays as afterschool and summer programs for quite some time. Many people have asked what the program is, therefore, I have put together a basic formula so any teacher or parent can follow and have melodramatic success! As well, many teachers use my books in a variety of ways. You can view the formula and many more resources on my website at: PlayingWithPlays.com

- Brendan

OTHER PLAYS AND FULL LENGTH SCRIPTS

We have over 30 different titles, as well as a full-length play in 4-acts for theatre groups: Shakespeare's Hilarious Tragedies. You can see all of our other titles on our website here: PlayingWithPlays.com/books

As well, you can see a sneak peek at some of those titles at the back of this book.

And, if you ever have any questions, please don't hesitate to ask at: Contact@PlayingWithPlays.com

LICENSES AND ROYALTIES

All performances and other productions require the issuance of a license. Here are the basic guidelines:

1) Please contact us! We always LOVE to hear about a school or group performing our books! We would also love to share photos and brag about your program as well! (with your permission, of course)

2) We require that you purchase a copy of the play for the director/teacher and each kid in the show.

3) If you are a group and DO NOT charge your kids to be in the production, contact us about our educational rates to get a copy in each kid's hands inexpensively. (we will make this work for you!)

4) If you are a group and DO charge your kids to be in the production, (i.e. afterschool program, summer camp), contact us for bulk (10 books or more) or educator's discounts.

5) If you are a group and DO NOT charge the audience to see the plays, please see our website FAQs (www.PlayingWithPlays.com) to see if you are eligible to waive the performance license(s) (most performances are eligible).

6) If you are a group and DO charge the audience to see the performance, please see our website FAQs for performance licensing fees (this includes performances for donations and competitions).

Any other questions or comments, please see our website or email us at:

contact@PlayingWithPlays.com

The 15-Minute or so THE WONDERFUL WIZARD OF OZ for Kids

by L. Frank Baum
Creatively modified by
Brendan P. Kelso
8-11 Actors

CAST OF CHARACTERS:

DOROTHY'S GANG

DOROTHY: a girl with a dog who gets lost in a tornado
SCARECROW: a bunch of hay without a brain
TIN WOODMAN: metal man without a heart
COWARDLY LION: king of beasts who's not so kingly

THE OTHERS

WICKED WITCH OF THE WEST: (WWW) the wickedest of witches
[1]**GOOD WITCH OF THE NORTH:** Good Witch from the north
[2]**MUNCHKIN:** a little person
[2]**OZ:** the good (or is it terrible?) wizard!
[3]**WINKIE:** slave of WWW
[3]**GLINDA:** Good Witch from the south
[1]**MONKEY:** leader of the winged monkeys

NONSPEAKING and EXTRA ROLES:
WICKED WITCH OF THE EAST: legs with funny looking stockings (can be a role or a prop)
RANDOM MUNCHKINS
FLYING MONKEYS
TOWNSFOLK OF THE EMERALD CITY
all these parts have no lines, but you can add some if you like!

The same actors can play the following parts:

[1]**GOOD NORTH WITCH and MONKEY**
[2]**MUNCHKIN and OZ**
[3]**WINKIE and GLINDA**

ACT 1 SCENE 1

(enter DOROTHY, carrying dog in basket, looking out)

DOROTHY: Another drab and dreary day on the Kansas prairie, Toto. Oh no! There's a cyclone coming. Aunt Em! Toto, let's leave the house! *(as she tries to exit, she starts spinning)* Woahhhhh!!!

(DOROTHY spins then passes out)

ACT 1 SCENE 2

(DOROTHY wakes)
DOROTHY: Toto, I don't think this is Kansas.
(enter NORTH WITCH and MUNCHKIN)
DOROTHY: You're such a curious little person.
MUNCHKIN: Who you calling little?
DOROTHY: Ummm, you?
MUNCHKIN: Oh, well then, yeah.
DOROTHY: Are there more of you?
MUNCHKIN: Yeah! They are all backstage. Listen!
MUNCHKINS: HELLO!
DOROTHY: Hello!
NORTH WITCH: Is your name Dorothy?
DOROTHY: Why, yes it is. How did you know?
NORTH WITCH: I'm a witch, I know things.
DOROTHY: Aren't witches ugly?
NORTH WITCH: *(strikes a pose)* Do I look ugly to you?
DOROTHY: No. You do not!
NORTH WITCH: Wicked witches are ugly.
MUNCHKIN: Like the one you killed, the Wicked Witch of the East!
DOROTHY: I have not killed anything. I wouldn't harm a fly!

NORTH WITCH: Well, your house did. See! There are her two feet. You have freed the Munchkins!

MUNCHKINS: Yay! *(starts Dorothy chant)*

DOROTHY: But where's Aunt Em? Where's Kansas?

MUNCHKIN: Kansas? Aunt Em? Those are funny sounding things.

DOROTHY: That's my home and family!

MUNCHKIN: Oh, wow, good luck getting there!

DOROTHY: But why?

NORTH WITCH: You are in the land of Oz surrounded by a great desert.

DOROTHY: But, how do I find Kansas?

NORTH WITCH: Perhaps the great Wizard of Oz can help?

DOROTHY: The wizard of who?

MUNCHKIN: The Wizard of Oz!

DOROTHY: How do I find him?

MUNCHKIN: You follow the road paved with yellow bricks to the City of Emeralds! But, before you go, be sure to take those silver shoes!

DOROTHY: You want me to wear another person's shoes? That's rather gross.

MUNCHKIN: They contain magic.

DOROTHY: Oh! Well why didn't you say so! *(puts on slippers)* But, shouldn't these be like... ruby slippers?

NORTH WITCH: No. Just silver.

DOROTHY: Are you sure?

NORTH WITCH: Let me check. *(pulls out Wizard of Oz book)* Yep. Silver. Remember, this play is based off the book, NOT the movie.

DOROTHY: Oh, that's right.

NORTH WITCH: And here, I give you my magic mark. *(gives "magic mark" as defined by director)*

MUNCHKIN: Now, no one will dare injure you!

DOROTHY: Well, that's good!

NORTH WITCH: Yes it is, now on your way!

DOROTHY: Oh right, the yellow brick road!

MUNCHKINS: The yellow brick road!

NORTH WITCH: Bye! *(NORTH WITCH exits)*

DOROTHY: Bye! *(exits)*

MUNCHKINS: Bye!

MUNCHKIN: *(to audience)* I hope she makes it. Remember, we don't just call Oz wonderful, we also referred to him as... **TERRIBLE!**

(ALL backstage say, "Dun-dun-dun!"; ALL exit)

ACT 1 SCENE 4

(TIN enters and poses with axe center upstage; moments later, SCARECROW and DOROTHY enter, look around)

SCARECROW: What a dark forest.

(TIN moans)

DOROTHY: What was that?

SCARECROW: *(looking around)* I cannot imagine!

(TIN moans again)

DOROTHY: I think it's coming from this Tin Woodman.

TIN: *(mumbles)* Oiiiiil.

DOROTHY: What did he say?

SCARECROW: He said, *(mimics TIN)*

DOROTHY: You are no help. Say it again, my rusted friend.

TIN: *(mumbles)* Oiiiiil.

DOROTHY: Oil! You said oil!

TIN: *(mumbles)* Yesssss!

SCARECROW: You speak tin man?

DOROTHY: Apparently so. Quick, get his oil-can.

(SCARECROW grabs oil can)

DOROTHY: His jaw! *(they oil his jaw)*

TIN: Thank you! Oil my neck, my arms, and my legs. *(walks around)* Oh, you have saved my life! Where are you headed?

DOROTHY: We are on our way to the Emerald City to see the Great Oz.

TIN: Why?

DOROTHY: To send me back to Kansas and give him brains.

TIN: Kansas? Brains? Hmmm? Do you suppose Oz could give me a heart?

DOROTHY: Well, if he can do those, then I'm sure a heart is no problem!

TIN: Well then, can I join you?

SCARECROW: Sure, come along! But tell me, why would you want a heart instead of a brain?

TIN: It's a story about a girl.

SCARECROW: Ahhh, say no more! I can understand that even **WITHOUT** a brain!

DOROTHY: Well then, are we off to see the Wizard?

TIN & SCARECROW: Yes!

(they hold hands and skip offstage)

ACT 1 SCENE 5

SCARECROW: We have to be careful in this forest.
TIN: W-w-w-why? W-w-w-what's here?
SCARECROW: Lions.
TIN: A-a-and?
SCARECROW: Tigers.
TIN: And?
SCARECROW: Bears!
DOROTHY: Oh, my! Lions, and tigers and...
(LION enters, roaring)
LION: Did you say lions?
DOROTHY: Well yes, but...
(roars again; DOROTHY bops LION)
LION: Ouch! What did you do that for?
DOROTHY: I was just about to break into a song.
LION: Oh, sorry. Please, go on.
DOROTHY: It's too late, you've ruined the moment.
LION: But, isn't this a musical?
DOROTHY: It was until you ruined it.
LION: Sorry.

DOROTHY: Don't apologize to me. Apologize to them... *(points to audience)*

LION: T-t-to them? But they're sc-c-cary!

TIN: Them? They're ordinary and dull looking.

SCARECROW: Especially that one. *(to LION)* What are you, a coward?

LION: Yes. Yes, I am. I'm a cowardly lion.

SCARECROW: Well, maybe the wizard can help you?

LION: The wizard?

TIN: That's a smart idea, Scarecrow! Yes, we are going to see the wizard for brains and a heart and something called Kansas!

DOROTHY: It's not a thing, it's my home!

LION: Do you think the wizard can give me courage?

DOROTHY: I don't see why not.

LION: Well then, do you mind if I join you? I'll roar very loudly to protect you!

SCARECROW: That would be wonderful!

TIN: Then we are off to see the wizard!

ALL: The wonderful Wizard of Oz!

(they skip around stage then slow down)

TIN: *(steps on something)* Uh, oh! *(looks under shoe)* Oh, no!!! I killed a poor little beetle! *(starts crying)*

SCARECROW: I'm sorry, Tin man.

DOROTHY: It's going to be okay.

(TIN'S jaw rusts, he frantically motions towards his face)

LION: Charades?! Oh, I love charades!

SCARECROW: You're eating something?

DOROTHY: Your mouth!

LION: No! Teeth! Tongue!

SCARECROW: I know! Jaws! *(acts like shark; TIN, frustrated, points at oilcan)*

DOROTHY: Oh! You rusted again!

(TIN nods; DOROTHY oils)

TIN: Finally!

SCARECROW: *(looking offstage)* Hey guys, look! It's the Emerald City!

(ALL cheer and exit)

ACT 2 SCENE 1

(ALL enter - giant floating head is opposite, OZ's voice is heard but not seen)

SCARECROW: I think this is the way. Come on everyone!

TIN: Whoa! That's a big noggin!

LION: That's a s-c-c-cary noggin!

OZ: WHO DARES TO COME SEE THE GREAT OZ!

DOROTHY: We have, your greatness.

OZ: WHY?!?!?!

DOROTHY: Well, it's pretty simple, really. We need a few upgrades. A brain, a heart, some courage, a trip home. You know, the total package.

OZ: If you want something from me, then you will have to do something for me in return!

SCARECROW: In return? Don't you have everything?

TIN: *(looking through DOROTHY'S basket)* Let's see, we have some nuts, a couple of apples, a dog.

DOROTHY: Tin man!

TIN: Oh, sorry. I guess the dog's off the table.

SCARECROW: You must have a ton of brains in that enormous head of yours! Can't you spare some?

OZ: NOOOOOO *(LION hides behind everyone)*

DOROTHY: Please, sir, we need some help!

OZ: Very well. A QUEST! Destroy the Wicked Witch of the West. Then, AND ONLY THEN, will I grant these things to you.

DOROTHY: But, sir...

OZ: NO BUTS! LEAVE! Before I decide to turn... terrible!

(LION scampers off stage, others follow; ALL exit)

ACT 2 SCENE 2

(WICKED enters cackling with telescope; looks out)

WICKED: What's this? Who dares come upon my land! Oh, Winkie!

(WINKIE enter, scared)

WINKIE: Y-y-yes...

WICKED: Go get them.

WINKIE: M-m-me?

WICKED: Y-y-yes, you! NOW GO!

(WINKIE runs offstage, LION roars! WINKIE runs on, across, and offstage, screaming!)

WICKED: *(to audience)* Pathetic. Am I right? Time for the winged monkeys!

(pulls out Golden Cap, says magic words; MONKEY enter)

MONKEY: You called? What do you need?

WICKED: Destroy that group and bring me the lion. I'll make him work.

MONKEY: Your order is our command.

WICKED: Great. Now go!

(MONKEY flies off, WITCH exits cackling)

ACT 2 SCENE 3

LION: Did you hear my fantastic roar!

DOROTHY: You were so brave!

(MONKEYS heard offstage)

LION: W-w-what's that noise?

TIN: Whatever it is, I'll get them with my axe!

SCARECROW: Oh no! It's the...

ALL: WINGED MONKEYS!

(MONKEY enters; everyone scrambles around; MONKEY grabs SCARECROW, TIN, and LION, and take them offstage separately; DOROTHY remains center)

DOROTHY: You are an awful, awful monkey! I hope they put you in a zoo!

(MONKEY grabs DOROTHY)

MONKEY: What is this? You have a magical mark upon you.

DOROTHY: I do. Now stand back!

MONKEY: Well, I can't kill this one, so I'll bring her back to the witch.

DOROTHY: Unhand me, you flea-riddled cretins!

MONKEY: There, there, this isn't personal. Just business.

(MONKEY takes DOROTHY offstage)

ACT 2 SCENE 4

(MONKEY enters with LION and DOROTHY; WICKED enters opposite)

WICKED: Take the Lion away! And why isn't she dead?!

MONKEY: You see the mark? *(WICKED looks)* Yeah, that.

WICKED: I also see those shoes. NIIICE!!! They will go well with my shoe collection.

DOROTHY: Okay, that's it. You can shred the scarecrow, you can ruin the tin man, you can even cage the lion, but gloves are coming off if you're going to take my shoes!

WICKED: Okay, you're right. My bad. Oh, would you look at that! *(points opposite)*

DOROTHY: *(looks away)* What?

WICKED: *(grabs for shoes)* They're mine!

DOROTHY: Get away!!!

WICKED: Fine! Then mop these floors. NOW!

DOROTHY: You're so mean!

WICKED: Yes. Yes, I am! *(cackles)*

(DOROTHY exits; MONKEY exits with LION)

WICKED: *(to audience)* I'll get those shoes, yet! My closet demands it!!! And, of course, they're magical!

(DOROTHY returns with sponge and bucket)

WICKED: You see this area? Mop it all!

DOROTHY: You are cruel.

WICKED: Yes, yes, yes. I've heard them all. Wicked, cruel, vicious, smelly.

DOROTHY: Smelly?

WICKED: Don't ask. Now, clean!

(DOROTHY cleans on knees downstage facing away from WICKED)

WICKED: There you go, over there a bit more.

(WICKED sneaks up behind DOROTHY, pretends to be looking at her mopping; creative fun could be had with this interchange; then finally grabs one shoe from DOROTHY'S feet)

WICKED: Ha, ha! It's mine!!

DOROTHY: What?! How dare you! *(picks up bucket and throws water at WICKED who gives loud cry of fear and begins melting away; WINKIE and LION enter)*

WICKED: See what you have done!

DOROTHY: Whoops! I'm very sorry indeed!

WICKED: Sorry?! But I'm mellltttttiiiinnnggg!

DOROTHY: Well, next time, don't touch my shoes! Ding-dong!

WICKED: Aghhhhhhhhhhhhhhhhhhhhhhhhhhhhhh!!!! *(dies)*

(ALL cheer)

DOROTHY: Winkie, you are now free!

(ALL cheer)

LION: But, I am sad. Our friends are now gone.

WINKIE: I can help you. I saw where the monkeys dumped them.

DOROTHY: You would help us?

WINKIE: Oh yes!

DOROTHY: Oh please, please. Thank you!

(WINKIE exits)

LION: Oh, I hope they find them!

(WINKIE enters with TIN and SCARECROW; ALL hug)

DOROTHY: This is so wonderful! But, we must go back to Oz, and claim his promise.

TIN: Yes! At last, I shall get my heart!

SCARECROW: And I shall get my brains.

LION: And I shall get my courage.

DOROTHY: And I shall get back to Kansas.

ALL: Yay!

WINKIE: Can't the tin man stay? He's shiny, and we want him to rule over us!

TIN: Ah, you're cute. But we must go back. I need my heart.

WINKIE: Okay, but take the Golden Cap. With it, you can call the winged monkeys!

DOROTHY: Really?!

WINKIE: Sure! Try it! Say the magic words inside the hat.

DOROTHY: Ok, here I go! *(says magical words; MONKEY flies onstage)*

MONKEY: What is your command?

DOROTHY: We wish to go to the Emerald City.

MONKEY: Well, buckle up!

ALL: Bye!

(ALL exit)

ACT 3 SCENE 1

(enter DOROTHY and gang; enter OZ opposite)
DOROTHY: Hello. We are here to see the wizard.
OZ: Wow! You came back?
SCARECROW: Do we know you?
OZ: Oh, ummm... I'm the guard, yeah. That's who I am!
TIN: Why wouldn't we come back?
OZ: I just thought... ahhh... well... never mind.
SCARECROW: You thought she would kill us?
OZ: Maybe? Or maybe do her bidding?
DOROTHY: Well, we melted her. Let Oz know we're here to collect!
OZ: Okey-dokey! *(exits; returns moments later)* Soooo, he said he needs to think about it, and he'll see you tomorrow. And when I say tomorrow, I mean he will keep blowing you off for like a week or two. So, just go on your way!
LION: What?! Tell him we will see him NOW!
OZ: All right, all right! Pushy... *(leads them around stage)* Here we are!
SCARECROW: Where is he?
OZ: He's everywhere! *(motions all around)* Okay, later! *(exits, but peeks out from behind curtain, not seen by others, but is seen by audience)*
DOROTHY: Hello?
OZ: HELLO!!! I am Oz, the Great and Terrible. Why do you seek me?

DOROTHY: We did what you asked. The Wicked Witch was destroyed.

TIN: We have come to claim our promise, O Oz.

OZ: Promise? What promise?

SCARECROW: Are you kidding us?

OZ: Well, come to me tomorrow, I need to think it over.

DOROTHY: Tomorrow? Oh, no you don't.

SCARECROW: We shan't wait a day longer.

TIN: You must keep your promises!

OZ: Yessss, I just need a bit more...

LION: ROARRRRRRRR!!!!

(everyone jumps back scared, DOROTHY notices OZ and pulls him onstage)

DOROTHY: Who are you? Aren't you the guard?

OZ: No. I am Oz, the great and terrible.

TIN: You seem more like a wazzz.

OZ: I suppose you're right. I'm just a common man.

DOROTHY: Common man? Where are you from?

OZ: I was born in Omaha.

SCARECROW: Ooh, sounds exotic.

TIN: Like a tropical beach!

LION: Or an island!

DOROTHY: Omaha!

TIN: *(to LION and SCARECROW)* I'm guessing not exotic.

DOROTHY: You are a very bad man!

OZ: Oh, no, my dear; I'm really a very good man, but I'm a very bad wizard.

DOROTHY: Okay, Mr. Omaha, how are you going to help us?

SCARECROW: Yes, I want my brains!

TIN: And my heart!

LION: And my c-c-c-courage.

OZ: You know, I think I can help you.

DOROTHY: And Kansas?

OZ: I should have an answer for that as well.

TIN: When can we start?

OZ: Now! Give me a moment. *(goes back stage and returns with "stuff"; DOROTHY and gang share excitement)* You realize the qualities you seek, you have possessed all along. But, as a symbolic gesture, please come sit. *(motions SCARECROW to chair)*

SCARECROW: My brains?

OZ: Your brains.

SCARECROW: I'm soooo excited!!! *(sits in chair facing audience; others watch; OZ winks at audience, pulls "brain" out of his bag)*

ALL: Oooooh.

OZ: Now sit back. *(sleight-of-hand hides "brain")* a little in here. *(places "brain" under hat)* And there you go. A head with brains!

ALL: Ahhhhhh.

DOROTHY: How do you feel?

SCARECROW: I feel wise indeed. Ask me a question!

TIN: What is the world record for the most socks put on one foot in one minute? *(or some other random fact)*

SCARECROW: 52!

(everyone cheers)

TIN: I'm next!

OZ: *(pulls out a symbolic heart)* Isn't it a beauty?

TIN: It is, indeed! But is it a kind heart?

OZ: Oh, very! I'll need to place it on your chest, is that okay?

TIN: Yes!

(OZ places heart on TIN)

OZ: There, now you have a heart any might be proud of.

TIN: Oh, thank you! Thank you!

OZ: Lion?

LION: P-p-please!

(pulls out bottle with liquid)

OZ: Drink.

LION: What is it?

OZ: Consider it... liquid courage.

LION: People drink this?

OZ: All the time. Remember, courage is always inside one. The sooner you drink, the sooner you will have your courage.

LION: Ok, bottoms up. For courage!
ALL: Courage!
(LION drinks)
OZ: How do you feel now?
LION: Full of courage! *(roars proudly)*
DOROTHY: And Kansas?
OZ: Balloon!
DOROTHY: Balloon?
OZ: Balloon.
SCARECROW: *(looks at others)* I'm the smart one, and I don't even get that.
OZ: We will fly out of here by balloon!
DOROTHY: Yay!
OZ: Mr. Brains, I leave you in charge.
SCARECROW: Yes!
OZ: My balloon is just over there, let's go!
(DOROTHY and OZ exit)
TIN: They didn't even say goodbye! *(starts crying)*
LION: Don't rust, Tin man!
SCARECROW: I hope they finally get home!
(TOTO is tossed onstage; DOROTHY chases)
DOROTHY: Toto! Don't run away!
LION: Oh, you're back already! Yay!
OZ: *(from backstage)* Goodbye!

DOROTHY: Nooooooooooooooooooo!!!! He left us. *(melodramatically sobs)*

LION: Oh, that's a bummer.

TIN: There, there, Dorothy. I'm sure there's another way.

DOROTHY: But I just want to go to Kansas!

SCARECROW: I know who could help us! Why not call the winged monkeys?

DOROTHY: Oh, yes!

LION: Wow, you are smart.

SCARECROW: Thank you!

(enter MONKEY)

TIN: That was fast.

MONKEY: Short play.

DOROTHY: Can you take me back to Kansas?

MONKEY: Sorry, can't cross the desert. Well, our work is done here. Later.

(MONKEY exits)

DOROTHY: Well, that stinks!

SCARECROW: I know! Glinda the Good Witch!

(MONKEY enters)

MONKEY: You need me again, don't you?

DOROTHY: Can you take us to Glinda the Good Witch?

MONKEY: That I can do.

(MONKEY carries everyone offstage)

ACT 3 SCENE 2

(MONKEY brings everyone onstage, GLINDA enters opposite)

GLINDA: Hello. What can I do for you, my child? Nice shoes by the way.

SCARECROW: Dorothy here, needs to go home.

GLINDA: I can help. But you must give me the golden cap.

DOROTHY: Willingly! *(gives cap)* It didn't really go with my outfit.

GLINDA: What will you do when Dorothy has left?

SCARECROW: I'll return to the Emerald City and be their leader.

TIN: I will go to the land of the Winkies, and rule over them.

LION: I want to be the King of the Forest.

GLINDA: Very well, the winged monkey will take you.

LION, SCARECROW, & TIN: Thank you!

GLINDA: And my winged friend, you may keep the Golden Cap and be free for evermore.

MONKEY: Thank you. It sure was getting tiresome flying all these people around with no pay.

DOROTHY: You are certainly as good as you are beautiful! Buuuut, what about Kansas?!

GLINDA: Your silver shoes will carry you over the desert, and back home.

DOROTHY: What?! I could've gone home from the very beginning?

GLINDA: Certainly. But you wouldn't have had this wonderful adventure and helped your new friends.

DOROTHY: Well, okay, that's true! Oh, I am so going to miss you all!

(ALL hug; TIN sobbing)

SCARECROW: Be careful Tin Man, you might rust again.

TIN: I know, it's this gosh darn heart!

GLINDA: Now Dorothy, all you have to do is to knock the heels together three times and command the shoes to carry you wherever you wish to go.

DOROTHY: *(clicks heels together)* Take me home to Aunt Em! *(they start spinning and fall asleep while MONKEY exits with LION, TIN, and SCARECROW; GLINDA exits; DOROTHY wakes, looks around)*

DOROTHY: Home! *(to audience)* Wow! The Land of Oz. What a dream! But, I'm so glad to be home again! There's no place like home! *(starts to exit)* That was a dream, right? *(thinks for a moment)* Right! Goodbye!

(exits)

THE END

NOTES

The 20-Minute or so THE WONDERFUL WIZARD OF OZ for Kids

by L. Frank Baum
Creatively modified by
Brendan P. Kelso
10-16 Actors

CAST OF CHARACTERS:

DOROTHY'S GANG

DOROTHY: a girl who gets lost in a tornado
TOTO: Dorothy's dog, a faithful companion who may or may not cause trouble
SCARECROW: a bunch of hay without a brain
[1]**TIN WOODMAN:** metal man without a heart
[2]**COWARDLY LION:** king of beasts who's not so kingly
[3]**AUNT EM:** the aunt!

THE OTHERS

[3]**WICKED WITCH OF THE WEST: (WWW)** the wickedest of witches
[4]**GOOD WITCH OF THE NORTH:** Good Witch from the north
[1]**MUNCHKIN 1:** a little person
[2]**MUNCHKIN 2:** another little person
[5]**GUARD OF THE EMERALD CITY:** a person with green whiskers
[6]**OZ:** the good (or is it terrible?) wizard!

[4]**WINKIE 1:** slave of WWW
[6]**WINKIE 2:** another forced to do WWW's bidding
[5]**GLINDA:** Good Witch from the south
MONKEY: leader of the winged monkeys

NONSPEAKING and EXTRA ROLES:
WICKED WITCH OF THE EAST: legs with funny looking stockings (can be a role or a prop)
RANDOM MUNCHKINS
FLYING MONKEYS
TOWNSFOLK OF THE EMERALD CITY
all these parts have no lines, but you can add some if you like!

The same actors can play the following parts:

[1]**MUNCHKIN and TIN WOODMAN**
[2]**LION and MUNCHKIN**
[3]**AUNT EM and WWW**
[4]**GOOD NORTH WITCH and WINKIE**
[5]**GUARD and GLINDA**
[6]**OZ and WINKIE**

PlayingWithPlays.com

ACT 1 SCENE 1

(enter DOROTHY carrying basket, EM, and TOTO)

EM: *(looking out)* Another drab and dreary day on the Kansas prairie, Dorothy.

DOROTHY: Yep. But excitement awaits. There's a cyclone coming, Aunt Em!

EM: Oh dear! Run for the cellar, Dorothy!

(EM runs offstage)

DOROTHY: Toto, let's leave the house! *(as they try to exit, TOTO starts spinning)*

TOTO: Roahhhhh!!!

DOROTHY: Toto! *(DOROTHY runs back and spins with TOTO; they both pass out)*

ACT 1 SCENE 2

(DOROTHY and TOTO wake)

DOROTHY: Toto, I don't think this is Kansas.

TOTO: Kansas? I'm not sure this is Earth!

DOROTHY: *(shocked)* You talk?

TOTO: *(to audience)* Ruh Roh! Barkity-bark! Munchkins!

(enter NORTH WITCH and MUNCHKINS; TOTO sniffs MUNCHKINS)

DOROTHY: You're such curious little people.

MUNCHKIN 1: Who you calling little?

DOROTHY: Ummm, you?

MUNCHKIN 2: Oh, well then, yeah.

NORTH WITCH: Is your name Dorothy?

DOROTHY: Why, yes it is. How did you know?

NORTH WITCH: I'm a witch, I know things.

DOROTHY: Aren't witches ugly?

NORTH WITCH: *(strikes a pose)* Do I look ugly to you?

DOROTHY: No. You do not!

NORTH WITCH: Wicked witches are ugly.

MUNCHKIN 1: Like the one you killed, the Wicked Witch of the East!

DOROTHY: I have not killed anything. I wouldn't harm a fly!

NORTH WITCH: Well, your house did. See! There are her two feet. You have freed the Munchkins!

MUNCHKINS: Yay! *(starts Dorothy chant)*

DOROTHY: But where's Aunt Em? Where's Kansas?

MUNCHKIN 2: Kansas?

MUNCHKIN 1: Aunt Em?

MUNCHKIN 2: Those are funny sounding things.

MUNCHKIN 1: She must have hit her head hard.

DOROTHY: That's my home and family!

MUNCHKIN 2: Oh, wow, good luck getting there!

DOROTHY: But why?

NORTH WITCH: You are in the land of Oz surrounded by a great desert.

DOROTHY: But, how do I find Kansas?

NORTH WITCH: Perhaps the great Wizard of Oz can help?

DOROTHY: The wizard of who?

MUNCHKIN 1: The Wizard of Oz!

DOROTHY: How do I find him?

MUNCHKIN 2: You follow the road paved with yellow bricks!

MUNCHKIN 1: To the City of Emeralds!

MUNCHKIN 2: But, before you go, be sure to take those silver shoes!

DOROTHY: You want me to wear another person's shoes? That's rather gross.

MUNCHKIN 1: They contain magic.

DOROTHY: Oh! Well why didn't you say so! *(puts on slippers)* But, shouldn't these be like... ruby slippers?

NORTH WITCH: No. Just silver.

DOROTHY: Are you sure?

NORTH WITCH: Let me check. *(pulls out Wizard of Oz book)* Yep. Silver. Remember, this play is based off the book, NOT the movie.

DOROTHY: Oh, that's right.

NORTH WITCH: And here, I give you my magic mark. *(gives "magic mark" as defined by director)*

MUNCHKIN 2: Now, no one will dare injure you!

DOROTHY: Well, that's good!

NORTH WITCH: Yes it is, now on your way!

DOROTHY: Oh right, the yellow brick road!

MUNCHKINS: The yellow brick road!

NORTH WITCH: Bye! *(NORTH WITCH exits)*

DOROTHY: Bye! *(exits with TOTO)*

MUNCHKINS: Bye!

MUNCHKIN 1: You think she'll make it?

MUNCHKIN 2: Eh, it's fifty-fifty. You know teenagers.

MUNCHKIN 1: Remember, we don't just call Oz wonderful, we also referred to him as... *(turns into audience)* TERRIBLE!

(ALL backstage say, "Dun-dun-dun!"; ALL exit)

ACT 1 SCENE 3

(SCARECROW enters, stands center upstage, poses; DOROTHY and TOTO enter, skips across stage and peeks at SCARECROW; when DOROTHY looks away, SCARECROW changes pose, DOROTHY looks back, curious; this repeats 1-3 more times, DOROTHY gets suspicious)

DOROTHY: *(to audience)* Excuse me, but is that scarecrow behind me... moving? It is, huh? I'll take a closer look.

(DOROTHY slowly walks up to SCARECROW who doesn't move, then...)

SCARECROW: Boo!!

DOROTHY: Aghhh!!!

TOTO: Raghhh!!!

DOROTHY: You scared us!

SCARECROW: Well, in my defense, my name does have scare in it.

DOROTHY: Wait, you talk?!

SCARECROW: Certainly! And if it wasn't for this pole, I'd be able to walk, too!

DOROTHY: I can help you with that! *(removes pole from SCARECROW; he stumbles)*

SCARECROW: I feel like new man! Thanks!

DOROTHY: What are you doing here?

SCARECROW: Until you came along, just hanging around.

DOROTHY: What are you going to do now?

SCARECROW: Dunno. Good question. Where are you going?

DOROTHY: Oh! I'm going to see the Wizard of Oz!

SCARECROW: Wizard?! He sounds smart!

DOROTHY: Oh, I'm sure he is! He's going to send me back to Kansas!

SCARECROW: Kansas? That's a weird name. Do you think he'd give me brains?

DOROTHY: Brains? You don't have any brains?

SCARECROW: Nope. Just straw. See!

DOROTHY: Wow. He might. Why don't you come?

SCARECROW: But what if he can't give me brains?

DOROTHY: Well, you'll be no worse off than you are now. And, believe me, there are many people WITH brains who don't know how to use them. So don't sell yourself short.

SCARECROW: Sounds great! Where do we go?

DOROTHY: We follow the yellow brick road!

SCARECROW: The yellow brick road?

DOROTHY: Yes! The yellow brick road! Come on!

(they exit skipping offstage)

ACT 1 SCENE 4

(TIN enters and poses with axe center upstage; moments later, SCARECROW and DOROTHY enter, look around)

SCARECROW: What a dark forest.

(TIN moans)

DOROTHY: What was that?

SCARECROW: *(looking around)* I cannot imagine!

(TIN moans again)

DOROTHY: I think it's coming from this Tin Woodman.

TIN: *(mumbles)* Oiiiiil.

(TOTO growls and bites TIN'S leg, but hurts mouth)

TOTO: Rrr-oww-eee!!! *(hides behind DOROTHY)*

DOROTHY: Silly dog. What did he say?

SCARECROW: He said, *(mimics TOTO)*

DOROTHY: Not the dog, the Tin Woodman.

SCARECROW: Oh, he said, *(mimics TIN)*

DOROTHY: You are no help. Say it again, my rusted friend.

TIN: *(mumbles)* Oiiiiil.

DOROTHY: Oil! You said oil!

TIN: *(mumbles)* Yesssss!

SCARECROW: You speak tin man?

DOROTHY: Apparently so. Quick, get his oil-can.

(SCARECROW grabs oil can)

DOROTHY: His jaw! *(they oil his jaw)*

TIN: Thank you! Oil my neck, my arms, and my legs. *(walks around)* Oh, you have saved my life! Where are you headed?

DOROTHY: We are on our way to the Emerald City to see the Great Oz.

TIN: Why?

DOROTHY: To send me back to Kansas and give him brains.

TIN: Kansas? Brains? Hmmm? Do you suppose Oz could give me a heart?

DOROTHY: Well, if he can do those, then I'm sure a heart is no problem!

TIN: Well then, can I join you?

SCARECROW: Sure, come along! But tell me, why would you want a heart instead of a brain?

TIN: It's a story about a girl.

SCARECROW: Ahhh, say no more! I can understand that even WITHOUT a brain!

DOROTHY: Well then, are we off to see the Wizard?

TIN & SCARECROW: Yes!

(they hold hands and skip offstage)

ACT 1 SCENE 5

SCARECROW: We have to be careful in this forest.
TIN: W-w-w-why? W-w-w-what's here?
SCARECROW: Lions.
TIN: A-a-and?
SCARECROW: Tigers.
TIN: And?
SCARECROW: Bears!
DOROTHY: Oh, my! Lions, and tigers and...
(LION enters, roaring)
LION: Did you say lions?
DOROTHY: Well yes, but...
(roars again; DOROTHY bops LION)
LION: Ouch!
TOTO: Ruh Roh!
LION: What did you do that for?
DOROTHY: I was just about to break into a song.
LION: Oh, sorry. Please, go on.
DOROTHY: It's too late, you've ruined the moment.
LION: But, isn't this a musical?
DOROTHY: It was until you ruined it.
LION: Sorry.

DOROTHY: Don't apologize to me. Apologize to them... *(points to audience)*

LION: T-t-to them? But they're sc-c-cary!

TIN: Them? They're ordinary and dull looking.

SCARECROW: Especially that one. *(to LION)* What are you, a coward?

LION: Yes. Yes, I am. I'm a cowardly lion.

SCARECROW: Well, maybe the wizard can help you?

LION: The wizard?

TIN: That's a smart idea, Scarecrow! Yes, we are going to see the wizard for brains and a heart and something called Kansas!

DOROTHY: It's not a thing, it's my home!

LION: Do you think the wizard can give me courage?

DOROTHY: I don't see why not.

LION: Well then, do you mind if I join you? I'll roar very loudly to protect you!

SCARECROW: That would be wonderful!

TIN: Then we are off to see the wizard!

ALL: The wonderful Wizard of Oz!

(they skip around stage then slow down)

TIN: *(steps on something)* Uh, oh! *(looks under shoe)* Oh, no!!! I killed a poor little beetle! *(starts crying)*

SCARECROW: I'm sorry, Tin man.

DOROTHY: It's going to be okay.

(TIN'S jaw rusts, he frantically motions towards his face)

LION: Charades?! Oh, I love charades!

SCARECROW: You're eating something?

DOROTHY: Your mouth!

LION: No! Teeth! Tongue!

SCARECROW: I know! Jaws! *(acts like shark; TIN, frustrated, points at oilcan)*

DOROTHY: Oh! You rusted again!

(TIN nods; DOROTHY oils)

TIN: Finally!

SCARECROW: *(looking offstage)* Hey guys, look! It's the Emerald City!

(ALL cheer and exit)

ACT 2 SCENE 1

(DOROTHY and gang enter, GUARD enters opposite)

GUARD: I am the guard of the Emerald City. What do you wish?

DOROTHY: We came here to see the Great Oz.

GUARD: Why do you wish to see the Terrible Oz?

DOROTHY: Wait, I'm confused. Is he great or is he terrible?

GUARD: Yes.

SCARECROW: Yes? Yes, he's great, or yes, he's terrible?

GUARD: Yes.

SCARECROW: I can see how you have never been promoted past doorman.

GUARD: Ouch. You're terrible. Listen, he's great, look at this city! But, if you come on a foolish errand, he can destroy you in an instant.

SCARECROW: Please. I need a brain.

TIN: And I need a heart.

LION: I need some courage! And she needs some Kansas.

TOTO: Rone? *(ALL look at TOTO curiously)*

DOROTHY: He wants a bone.

GUARD: Fiiiiine. I will ask, but no guarantees.

DOROTHY: Oh and tell him I have these really cool shoes!

(GUARD looks, goes offstage, then returns)

SCARECROW: Well?

GUARD: Those silver slippers sold him and that magical mark upon you has him very curious. Come with me.

(ALL exit cheering)

ACT 2 SCENE 2

(ALL enter - giant floating head is opposite, OZ's voice is heard but not seen)

TIN: Whoa! That's a big noggin!

LION: That's a s-c-c-cary noggin!

OZ: WHO DARES TO COME SEE THE GREAT OZ!

DOROTHY: We have, your greatness.

OZ: WHY?!?!?!

DOROTHY: Well, it's pretty simple, really. We need a few upgrades. A brain, a heart, some courage, a trip home. You know, the total package.

OZ: If you want something from me, then you will have to do something for me in return!

SCARECROW: In return? Don't you have everything?

TIN: *(looking through DOROTHY'S basket)* Let's see, we have some nuts, a couple of apples, a dog.

TOTO: RUH?!

DOROTHY: Tin man!

TIN: Oh, sorry. I guess the dog's off the table.

SCARECROW: You must have a ton of brains in that enormous head of yours! Can't you spare some?

OZ: NOOOOOO *(LION hides behind everyone)*

TOTO: Rog rones?!

OZ: ENOUGH!

DOROTHY: Please, sir, we need some help!

OZ: Very well. A QUEST! Destroy the Wicked Witch of the West. Then, AND ONLY THEN, will I grant these things to you.

DOROTHY: But, sir...

OZ: NO BUTS! LEAVE! Before I decide to turn... terrible!

(LION scampers off stage, others follow; ALL exit)

ACT 2 SCENE 3

(WICKED enters cackling with telescope; looks out)

WICKED: What's this? Who dares come upon my land! Oh, Winkies!

(WINKIES enter, scared)

WINKIE 1: Y-y-yes...

WICKED: Go get them.

WINKIE 2: Us?!

WICKED: Y-y-yes, you! NOW GO!

(WINKIES run offstage, LION roars! WINKIES run on, across, and offstage, screaming!)

WICKED: *(to audience)* Pathetic. Am I right? Time for the winged monkeys!

(pulls out Golden Cap, says magic words; MONKEYS enter)

MONKEY: You called? What do you need?

WICKED: Destroy that group and bring me the lion. I'll make him work.

MONKEY: Your order is our command.

WICKED: Great. Now go!

(MONKEYS fly off, WITCH exits cackling)

ACT 2 SCENE 4

LION: Did you hear my fantastic roar!

DOROTHY: You were so brave!

TOTO: *(agrees enthusiastically)* Ruh-Ruh!

(MONKEYS heard offstage)

LION: W-w-what's that noise?

TIN: Whatever it is, I'll get them with my axe!

SCARECROW: Oh no! It's the...

ALL: WINGED MONKEYS!

(MONKEYS enter; everyone scrambles around; MONKEYS grab SCARECROW, TIN, and LION, and take them offstage separately; DOROTHY and TOTO remain center)

DOROTHY: You are awful, awful monkeys! I hope they put you in a zoo!

(MONKEYS gather around DOROTHY and growling TOTO)

MONKEY: What is this? You have a magical mark upon you.

DOROTHY: I do. Now stand back!

MONKEY: Listen monkeys, we can't kill this one, so let's bring her back to the witch.

DOROTHY: Unhand me, you flea-riddled cretins!

MONKEY: There, there, this isn't personal. Just business.

(MONKEYS take DOROTHY and TOTO offstage)

ACT 2 SCENE 5

(MONKEYS enter with LION, DOROTHY, and TOTO; WICKED enters opposite)

WICKED: Take the Lion away! And why isn't she dead?!

MONKEY: You see the mark? *(WICKED looks)* Yeah, that.

WICKED: I also see those shoes. NIIICE!!! They will go well with my shoe collection.

DOROTHY: Okay, that's it. You can shred the scarecrow, you can ruin the tin man, you can even cage the lion, but gloves are coming off if you're going to take my shoes!

WICKED: Okay, you're right. My bad. Oh, would you look at that! *(points opposite)*

DOROTHY: *(looks away)* What?

WICKED: *(grabs for shoes)* They're mine!

DOROTHY: Get away!!! *(TOTO growls)*

WICKED: Fine! Then mop these floors. NOW!

DOROTHY: You're so mean!

WICKED: Yes. Yes, I am! *(cackles)*

(DOROTHY and TOTO exit; MONKEYS exit with LION)

WICKED: *(to audience)* I'll get those shoes, yet! My closet demands it!!! And, of course, they're magical!

(DOROTHY returns with sponge and bucket, TOTO to side)

WICKED: You see this area? Mop it all!

DOROTHY: You are cruel.

WICKED: Yes, yes, yes. I've heard them all. Wicked, cruel, vicious, smelly.

DOROTHY: Smelly?

WICKED: Don't ask. Now, clean!

(DOROTHY cleans on knees downstage facing away from WICKED)

WICKED: There you go, over there a bit more.

(WICKED sneaks up behind DOROTHY, pretends to be looking at her mopping; creative fun could be had with this interchange; then finally grabs one shoe from DOROTHY'S feet)

WICKED: Ha, ha! It's mine!!

DOROTHY: What?! How dare you! *(picks up bucket and throws water at WICKED who gives loud cry of fear and begins melting away; WINKIES and LION enter)*

WICKED: See what you have done!

DOROTHY: Whoops! I'm very sorry indeed!

WICKED: Sorry?! But I'm mellltttttiiiinnnggg!

DOROTHY: Well, next time, don't touch my shoes! Ding-dong!

WICKED: Aghhhhhhhhhhhhhhhhhhhhhhhhhhhhhhh!!!! *(dies)*

(ALL cheer)

DOROTHY: Winkies, you are now free!

(ALL cheer)

LION: But, I am sad. Our friends are now gone.

WINKIE 1: We can help you.

WINKIE 2: Yes, we can rescue them.

WINKIE 1: We saw where the monkeys dumped them.

DOROTHY: You would help us?

WINKIES: Oh yes!

DOROTHY: Oh please, please. Thank you!

WINKIE 2: Let's go!

(WINKIES exit)

LION: Oh, I hope they find them!

(WINKIES enter with TIN and SCARECROW; ALL hug)

DOROTHY: This is so wonderful! But, we must go back to Oz, and claim his promise.

TIN: Yes! At last, I shall get my heart!

SCARECROW: And I shall get my brains.

LION: And I shall get my courage.

DOROTHY: And I shall get back to Kansas.

ALL: Yay!

TOTO: Rone?

DOROTHY: Maybe.

TOTO: Roh.

WINKIE 1: Can't the tin man stay?

WINKIE 2: Yes! He's shiny, and we want him to rule over us!

TIN: Ah, you guys are cute. But we must go back. I need my heart.

WINKIE 1: Okay, but take the Golden Cap. With it, you can call the winged monkeys!

DOROTHY: Really?!

WINKIE 2: Sure! Try it! Say the magic words inside the hat.

DOROTHY: Ok, here I go! *(says magical words; MONKEYS fly onstage)*

MONKEY: What is your command?

DOROTHY: We wish to go to the Emerald City.

MONKEY: Well, buckle up!

ALL: Bye!

(ALL exit)

ACT 3 SCENE 1

(enter DOROTHY and gang; enter GUARD opposite)

DOROTHY: We are here to see the wizard.

GUARD: Wow! You came back?

TIN: Of course, why wouldn't we?

GUARD: I just thought... ahhh... well... never mind.

SCARECROW: You thought she would kill us?

GUARD: Maybe? Or maybe do her bidding?

DOROTHY: Well, we melted her. Let Oz know we're here to collect!

GUARD: Okey-dokey! *(exits; returns moments later)* Sooooo, he said he needs to think about it, and he'll see you tomorrow. And when I say tomorrow, I mean he will keep blowing you off for like a week or two.

LION: What?! Tell him we will see him NOW!

GUARD: All right, all right! Pushy... *(leads them around stage)* Here we are!

SCARECROW: Where is he?

GUARD: He's everywhere! *(motions all around)* Okay, later! *(exits)*

(OZ peeks out from behind curtain, not seen by others, but is seen by audience)

DOROTHY: Hello?

OZ: HELLO!!! I am Oz, the Great and Terrible. Why do you seek me?

DOROTHY: We did what you asked. The Wicked Witch was destroyed.

TIN: We have come to claim our promise, O Oz.

OZ: Promise? What promise?

SCARECROW: Are you kidding us?

OZ: Well, come to me tomorrow, I need to think it over.

DOROTHY: Tomorrow? Oh, no you don't.

SCARECROW: We shan't wait a day longer.

TIN: You must keep your promises!

OZ: Yessss, I just need a bit more...

LION: ROARRRRRRRR!!!!

(everyone jumps back scared, TOTO runs offstage and pulls on OZ)

DOROTHY: Who are you?

OZ: I am Oz, the great and terrible? *(TOTO growls)*

TIN: You seem more like a wazzz.

OZ: I suppose you're right. I'm just a common man.

DOROTHY: Common man? Where are you from?

OZ: I was born in Omaha.

SCARECROW: Ooh, sounds exotic.

TIN: Like a tropical beach!

LION: Or an island!

DOROTHY: Omaha!

TIN: *(to LION and SCARECROW)* I'm guessing not exotic.

DOROTHY: You are a very bad man!

OZ: Oh, no, my dear; I'm really a very good man, but I'm a very bad wizard.

DOROTHY: Okay, Mr. Omaha, how are you going to help us?

SCARECROW: Yes, I want my brains!

TIN: And my heart!

LION: And my c-c-c-courage.

TOTO: Rone?

OZ: You know, I think I can help you.

DOROTHY: And Kansas?

OZ: I should have an answer for that as well.

TIN: When can we start?

OZ: Now! Give me a moment. *(goes back stage and returns with "stuff"; DOROTHY and gang share excitement)* You realize the qualities you seek, you have possessed all along. But, as a symbolic gesture, please come sit. *(motions SCARECROW to chair)*

SCARECROW: My brains?

OZ: Your brains.

SCARECROW: I'm soooo excited!!! *(sits in chair facing audience; others watch; OZ winks at audience, pulls "brain" out of his bag)*

ALL: Oooooh.

OZ: Now sit back. *(sleight-of-hand hides "brain")* a little in here. *(places "brain" under hat)* And there you go. A head with brains!

ALL: Ahhhhhh.

DOROTHY: How do you feel?

SCARECROW: I feel wise indeed. Ask me a question!

TIN: What is the world record for the most socks put on one foot in one minute? *(or some other random fact)*

SCARECROW: 52!

(everyone cheers)

TIN: I'm next!

OZ: *(pulls out a symbolic heart)* Isn't it a beauty?

TIN: It is, indeed! But is it a kind heart?

OZ: Oh, very! I'll need to place it on your chest, is that okay?

TIN: Yes!

(OZ places heart on TIN)

OZ: There, now you have a heart any might be proud of.

TIN: Oh, thank you! Thank you!

OZ: Lion?

LION: P-p-please!

(pulls out bottle with liquid)

OZ: Drink.

LION: What is it?

OZ: Consider it... liquid courage.

LION: People drink this?

OZ: All the time. Remember, courage is always inside one. The sooner you drink, the sooner you will have your courage.

LION: Ok, bottoms up. For courage!

ALL: Courage!

(LION drinks)

OZ: How do you feel now?

LION: Full of courage! *(roars proudly)*

DOROTHY: And Kansas?

OZ: Balloon!

DOROTHY: Balloon?

OZ: Balloon.

SCARECROW: *(looks at others)* I'm the smart one, and I don't even get that.

OZ: We will fly out of here by balloon!

DOROTHY: Yay!

OZ: Mr. Brains, I leave you in charge.

SCARECROW: Yes!

OZ: My balloon is just over there, let's go!

(DOROTHY, OZ, and TOTO exit)

TIN: They didn't even say goodbye! *(starts crying)*

LION: Don't rust, Tin man!

SCARECROW: I hope Toto finally gets his bone!

(TOTO runs across stage)

TOTO: Rone?

(DOROTHY chases)

DOROTHY: Toto!

LION: Oh, you're back already! Yay!

OZ: *(from backstage)* Goodbye!

DOROTHY: Nooooooooooooooooooo!!!! He left us. *(melodramatically sobs)*

LION: Oh, that's a bummer.

TIN: There, there, Dorothy. I'm sure there's another way.

DOROTHY: But I just want to go to Kansas!

SCARECROW: I know who could help us! Why not call the winged monkeys?

DOROTHY: Oh, yes!

LION: Wow, you are smart.

SCARECROW: Thank you!

(enter MONKEY)

TIN: That was fast.

MONKEY: Short play.

DOROTHY: Can you take me back to Kansas?

MONKEY: Sorry, can't cross the desert. Well, our work is done here. Later.

(MONKEYS exit)

DOROTHY: Well, that stinks!

SCARECROW: I know! Glinda the Good Witch!

(MONKEYS enter)

MONKEY: You need us again, don't you?

DOROTHY: Can you take us to Glinda the Good Witch?

MONKEY: That we can do.

(MONKEYS carry everyone offstage)

ACT 3 SCENE 2

(MONKEYS bring everyone onstage, GLINDA enters opposite)

GLINDA: Hello. What can I do for you, my child? Nice shoes by the way.

SCARECROW: Dorothy here, needs to go home.

GLINDA: I can help. But you must give me the golden cap.

DOROTHY: Willingly! *(gives cap)* It didn't really go with my outfit.

GLINDA: What will you do when Dorothy has left?

SCARECROW: I'll return to the Emerald City and be their leader.

TIN: I will go to the land of the Winkies, and rule over them.

LION: I want to be the King of the Forest.

GLINDA: Very well, the winged monkeys will take you.

LION, SCARECROW, & TIN: Thank you!

GLINDA: And my winged friends, you may keep the Golden Cap and be free for evermore.

MONKEY: Thank you. It sure was getting tiresome flying all these people around with no pay.

DOROTHY: You are certainly as good as you are beautiful! Buuuut, what about Kansas?!

GLINDA: Your silver shoes will carry you over the desert, and back home.

DOROTHY: What?! I could've gone home from the very beginning?

GLINDA: Certainly. But you wouldn't have had this wonderful adventure and helped your new friends.

DOROTHY: Well, okay, that's true! Oh, I am so going to miss you all!

(ALL hug; TIN sobbing)

SCARECROW: Be careful Tin Man, you might rust again.

TIN: I know, it's this gosh darn heart!

GLINDA: Now Dorothy, all you have to do is to knock the heels together three times and command the shoes to carry you wherever you wish to go.

DOROTHY: *(grabs TOTO, clicks heels together)* Take me home to Aunt Em! *(they start spinning and fall asleep while MONKEYS exit with LION, TIN, and SCARECROW; GLINDA exits; enter EM running to DOROTHY'S side; DOROTHY and TOTO wake)*

EM: My darling child! Where have you been?

DOROTHY: The Land of Oz. Nice new house, by the way.

EM: Thanks, the other blew away in that tornado.

DOROTHY: Yeah, I know. I'm so glad to be home again! There's no place like home!

EM: Come, child. Let's get you some food and that dog a bone.

TOTO: Roooohhh!!!!

(ALL exit)

THE END

NOTES

The 25-Minute or so THE WONDERFUL WIZARD OF OZ for Kids

by L. Frank Baum
Creatively modified by
Brendan P. Kelso
16-22+ Actors

CAST OF CHARACTERS:

DOROTHY'S GANG

DOROTHY: a girl who gets lost in a tornado
TOTO: Dorothy's dog, a faithful companion who may or may not cause trouble
SCARECROW: a bunch of hay without a brain
TIN WOODMAN: metal man without a heart
COWARDLY LION: king of beasts who's not so kingly
[1]**AUNT EM**: the aunt!
[2]**UNCLE HENRY**: the uncle!

THE OTHERS

[1]**WICKED WITCH OF THE WEST**: (WWW) the wickedest of witches
[3]**LEAD WOLF**: leader of the wolves
[4]**KING CROW**: leader of the crows
[5]**HEAD BEE**: leader of the bees
[4]**GOOD WITCH OF THE NORTH**: Good Witch from the north

[6]**MUNCHKIN 1**: a little person
[3]**MUNCHKIN 2**: another little person
[5]**MUNCHKIN 3**: yep, another!
[6]**GUARD OF THE EMERALD CITY**: a person with green whiskers
[2]**OZ**: the good (or is it terrible?) wizard!
WINKIE 1: slave of WWW
WINKIE 2: another forced to do WWW's bidding
WINKIE 3: and yet, poor thing, another
GLINDA: Good Witch from the south
MONKEY: leader of the winged monkeys

NONSPEAKING and EXTRA ROLES:
WICKED WITCH OF THE EAST: legs with funny looking stockings (can be a role or a prop)
BEES: buzzing killer bees
CROWS: cawing cruel crows
WOLVES: snarling deadly wolves
RANDOM MUNCHKINS
FLYING MONKEYS
TOWNSFOLK OF THE EMERALD CITY
all these parts have no lines, but you can add some if you like!

The same actors can play the following parts:

[1]**AUNT EM and WWW**
[2]**UNCLE HENRY and OZ**
[3]**MUNCHKIN and LEAD WOLF**
[4]**GOOD WITCH and KING CROW**
[5]**HEAD BEE and MUNCHKIN**
[6]**GUARD and MUNCHKIN**

ACT 1 SCENE 1

(enter DOROTHY carrying basket, EM, HENRY, and TOTO)

EM: *(looking out)* Another drab and dreary day on the Kansas prairie, Henry.

HENRY: Yep. But excitement awaits. There's a cyclone coming, Em!

EM: Oh dear! Run for the cellar, Dorothy!

(EM and HENRY run offstage)

DOROTHY: Toto, let's leave the house! *(as they try to exit, TOTO starts spinning)*

TOTO: Roahhhhh!!!

DOROTHY: Toto! *(DOROTHY runs back and spins with TOTO; they both pass out)*

ACT 1 SCENE 2

(DOROTHY and TOTO wake)

DOROTHY: Toto, I don't think this is Kansas.

TOTO: Kansas? I'm not sure this is Earth!

DOROTHY: *(shocked)* You talk?

TOTO: *(to audience)* Ruh Roh! Barkity-bark! Munchkins!

(enter NORTH WITCH and MUNCHKINS; TOTO sniffs MUNCHKINS)

DOROTHY: You're such curious little people.

MUNCHKIN 1: Who you calling little?

DOROTHY: Ummm, you?

MUNCHKIN 2: Oh, well then, yeah.

NORTH WITCH: Is your name Dorothy?

DOROTHY: Why, yes it is. How did you know?

NORTH WITCH: I'm a witch, I know things.

DOROTHY: Aren't witches ugly?

NORTH WITCH: *(strikes a pose)* Do I look ugly to you?

DOROTHY: No. You do not!

NORTH WITCH: Wicked witches are ugly.

MUNCHKIN 3: Like the one you killed, the Wicked Witch of the East!

DOROTHY: I have not killed anything. I wouldn't harm a fly!

NORTH WITCH: Well, your house did. See! There are her two feet. You have freed the Munchkins!

MUNCHKINS: Yay! *(starts Dorothy chant)*
DOROTHY: But where's Aunt Em? Where's Kansas?
MUNCHKIN 1: Kansas?
MUNCHKIN 2: Aunt Em?
MUNCHKIN 3: Those are funny sounding things.
MUNCHKIN 1: She must have hit her head hard.
DOROTHY: That's my home and family!
MUNCHKIN 2: Oh, wow, good luck getting there!
DOROTHY: But why?
NORTH WITCH: You are in the land of Oz surrounded by a great desert.
DOROTHY: But, how do I find Kansas?
NORTH WITCH: Perhaps the great Wizard of Oz can help?
DOROTHY: The wizard of who?
MUNCHKIN 1: The Wizard of Oz!
DOROTHY: How do I find him?
MUNCHKIN 2: You follow the road paved with yellow bricks!
MUNCHKIN 3: To the City of Emeralds!
MUNCHKIN 1: But, before you go, be sure to take those silver shoes!
DOROTHY: You want me to wear another person's shoes? That's rather gross.
MUNCHKIN 2: They contain magic.
DOROTHY: Oh! Well why didn't you say so! *(puts on slippers)* But, shouldn't these be like... ruby slippers?

NORTH WITCH: No. Just silver.

DOROTHY: Are you sure?

NORTH WITCH: Let me check. *(pulls out Wizard of Oz book)* Yep. Silver. Remember, this play is based off the book, NOT the movie.

DOROTHY: Oh, that's right.

NORTH WITCH: And here, I give you my magic mark. *(gives "magic mark" as defined by director)*

MUNCHKIN 3: Now, no one will dare injure you!

DOROTHY: Well, that's good!

NORTH WITCH: Yes it is, now on your way!

DOROTHY: Oh right, the yellow brick road!

MUNCHKINS: The yellow brick road!

NORTH WITCH: Bye! *(NORTH WITCH exits)*

DOROTHY: Bye! *(exits with TOTO)*

MUNCHKINS: Bye!

MUNCHKIN 1: You think she'll make it?

MUNCHKIN 2: Eh, it's fifty-fifty. You know teenagers.

MUNCHKIN 3: Remember, we don't just call Oz wonderful, we also referred to him as... *(turns into audience)* TERRIBLE!

(ALL backstage say, "Dun-dun-dun!"; ALL exit)

ACT 1 SCENE 3

(SCARECROW enters, stands center upstage, poses; DOROTHY and TOTO enter, skips across stage and peeks at SCARECROW; when DOROTHY looks away, SCARECROW changes pose, DOROTHY looks back, curious; this repeats 1-3 more times, DOROTHY gets suspicious)

DOROTHY: *(to audience)* Excuse me, but is that scarecrow behind me… moving? It is, huh? I'll take a closer look.

(DOROTHY slowly walks up to SCARECROW who doesn't move, then…)

SCARECROW: Boo!!

DOROTHY: Aghhh!!!

TOTO: Raghhh!!!

DOROTHY: You scared us!

SCARECROW: Well, in my defense, my name does have scare in it.

DOROTHY: Wait, you talk?!

SCARECROW: Certainly! And if it wasn't for this pole, I'd be able to walk, too!

DOROTHY: I can help you with that! *(removes pole from SCARECROW; he stumbles)*

SCARECROW: I feel like new man! Thanks!

DOROTHY: What are you doing here?

SCARECROW: Until you came along, just hanging around.

DOROTHY: What are you going to do now?

SCARECROW: Dunno. Good question. Where are you going?

DOROTHY: Oh! I'm going to see the Wizard of Oz!

SCARECROW: Wizard?! He sounds smart!

DOROTHY: Oh, I'm sure he is! He's going to send me back to Kansas!

SCARECROW: Kansas? That's a weird name. Do you think he'd give me brains?

DOROTHY: Brains? You don't have any brains?

SCARECROW: Nope. Just straw. See!

DOROTHY: Wow. He might. Why don't you come?

SCARECROW: But what if he can't give me brains?

DOROTHY: Well, you'll be no worse off than you are now. And, believe me, there are many people WITH brains who don't know how to use them. So don't sell yourself short.

SCARECROW: Sounds great! Where do we go?

DOROTHY: We follow the yellow brick road!

SCARECROW: The yellow brick road?

DOROTHY: Yes! The yellow brick road! Come on!

(they exit skipping offstage)

ACT 1 SCENE 4

(TIN enters and poses with axe center upstage; moments later, SCARECROW and DOROTHY enter, look around)

SCARECROW: What a dark forest.

(TIN moans)

DOROTHY: What was that?

SCARECROW: *(looking around)* I cannot imagine!

(TIN moans again)

DOROTHY: I think it's coming from this Tin Woodman.

TIN: *(mumbles)* Oiiiiil.

(TOTO growls and bites TIN'S leg, but hurts mouth)

TOTO: Rrr-oww-eee!!! *(hides behind DOROTHY)*

DOROTHY: Silly dog. What did he say?

SCARECROW: He said, *(mimics TOTO)*

DOROTHY: Not the dog, the Tin Woodman.

SCARECROW: Oh, he said, *(mimics TIN)*

DOROTHY: You are no help. Say it again, my rusted friend.

TIN: *(mumbles)* Oiiiiil.

DOROTHY: Oil! You said oil!

TIN: *(mumbles)* Yesssss!

SCARECROW: You speak tin man?

DOROTHY: Apparently so. Quick, get his oil-can.

(SCARECROW grabs oil can)

DOROTHY: His jaw! *(they oil his jaw)*

TIN: Thank you! Oil my neck, my arms, and my legs. *(walks around)* Oh, you have saved my life! Where are you headed?

DOROTHY: We are on our way to the Emerald City to see the Great Oz.

TIN: Why?

DOROTHY: To send me back to Kansas and give him brains.

TIN: Kansas? Brains? Hmmm? Do you suppose Oz could give me a heart?

DOROTHY: Well, if he can do those, then I'm sure a heart is no problem!

TIN: Well then, can I join you?

SCARECROW: Sure, come along! But tell me, why would you want a heart instead of a brain?

TIN: It's a story about a girl.

SCARECROW: Ahhh, say no more! I can understand that even WITHOUT a brain!

DOROTHY: Well then, are we off to see the Wizard?

TIN & SCARECROW: Yes!

(they hold hands and skip offstage)

ACT 1 SCENE 5

SCARECROW: We have to be careful in this forest.
TIN: W-w-w-why? W-w-w-what's here?
SCARECROW: Lions.
TIN: A-a-and?
SCARECROW: Tigers.
TIN: And?
SCARECROW: Bears!
DOROTHY: Oh, my! Lions, and tigers and...
(LION enters, roaring)
LION: Did you say lions?
DOROTHY: Well yes, but...
(roars again; DOROTHY bops LION)
LION: Ouch!
TOTO: Ruh Roh!
LION: What did you do that for?
DOROTHY: I was just about to break into a song.
LION: Oh, sorry. Please, go on.
DOROTHY: It's too late, you've ruined the moment.
LION: But, isn't this a musical?
DOROTHY: It was until you ruined it.
LION: Sorry.

DOROTHY: Don't apologize to me. Apologize to them... *(points to audience)*

LION: T-t-to them? But they're sc-c-cary!

TIN: Them? They're ordinary and dull looking.

SCARECROW: Especially that one. *(to LION)* What are you, a coward?

LION: Yes. Yes, I am. I'm a cowardly lion.

SCARECROW: Well, maybe the wizard can help you?

LION: The wizard?

TIN: That's a smart idea, Scarecrow! Yes, we are going to see the wizard for brains and a heart and something called Kansas!

DOROTHY: It's not a thing, it's my home!

LION: Do you think the wizard can give me courage?

DOROTHY: I don't see why not.

LION: Well then, do you mind if I join you? I'll roar very loudly to protect you!

SCARECROW: That would be wonderful!

TIN: Then we are off to see the wizard!

ALL: The wonderful Wizard of Oz!

(they skip around stage then slow down)

TIN: *(steps on something)* Uh, oh! *(looks under shoe)* Oh, no!!! I killed a poor little beetle! *(starts crying)*

SCARECROW: I'm sorry, Tin man.

DOROTHY: It's going to be okay.

(TIN'S jaw rusts, he frantically motions towards his face)

LION: Charades?! Oh, I love charades!

SCARECROW: You're eating something?

DOROTHY: Your mouth!

LION: No! Teeth! Tongue!

SCARECROW: I know! Jaws! *(acts like shark; TIN, frustrated, points at oilcan)*

DOROTHY: Oh! You rusted again!

(TIN nods; DOROTHY oils)

TIN: Finally!

SCARECROW: *(looking offstage)* Hey guys, look! It's the Emerald City!

(ALL cheer and exit)

ACT 2 SCENE 1

(DOROTHY and gang enter, GUARD enters opposite)

GUARD: I am the guard of the Emerald City. What do you wish?

DOROTHY: We came here to see the Great Oz.

GUARD: Why do you wish to see the Terrible Oz?

DOROTHY: Wait, I'm confused. Is he great or is he terrible?

GUARD: Yes.

SCARECROW: Yes? Yes, he's great, or yes, he's terrible?

GUARD: Yes.

SCARECROW: I can see how you have never been promoted past doorman.

GUARD: Ouch. You're terrible. Listen, he's great, look at this city! But, if you come on a foolish errand, he can destroy you in an instant.

SCARECROW: Please. I need a brain.

TIN: And I need a heart.

LION: I need some courage! And she needs some Kansas.

TOTO: Rone? *(ALL look at TOTO curiously)*

DOROTHY: He wants a bone.

GUARD: Fiiiiine. I will ask, but no guarantees.

DOROTHY: Oh and tell him I have these really cool shoes!

(GUARD looks, goes offstage, then returns)

SCARECROW: Well?

GUARD: Those silver slippers sold him and that magical mark upon you has him very curious. Come with me.

(ALL exit cheering)

ACT 2 SCENE 2

(ALL enter - giant floating head is opposite, OZ's voice is heard but not seen)

TIN: Whoa! That's a big noggin!

LION: That's a s-c-c-cary noggin!

OZ: WHO DARES TO COME SEE THE GREAT OZ!

DOROTHY: We have, your greatness.

OZ: WHY?!?!?!

DOROTHY: Well, it's pretty simple, really. We need a few upgrades. A brain, a heart, some courage, a trip home. You know, the total package.

OZ: If you want something from me, then you will have to do something for me in return!

SCARECROW: In return? Don't you have everything?

TIN: *(looking through DOROTHY'S basket)* Let's see, we have some nuts, a couple of apples, a dog.

TOTO: RUH?!

DOROTHY: Tin man!

TIN: Oh, sorry. I guess the dog's off the table.

SCARECROW: You must have a ton of brains in that enormous head of yours! Can't you spare some?

OZ: NOOOOOO *(LION hides behind everyone)*

TOTO: Rog rones?!

OZ: ENOUGH!

DOROTHY: Please, sir, we need some help!

OZ: Very well. A QUEST! Destroy the Wicked Witch of the West. Then, AND ONLY THEN, will I grant these things to you.

DOROTHY: But, sir...

OZ: NO BUTS! LEAVE! Before I decide to turn... terrible!

(LION scampers off stage, others follow; ALL exit)

ACT 2 SCENE 3

(WICKED enters cackling with telescope; looks out)

WICKED: What's this? Who dares come upon my land! *(whistles once; pause, WOLVES enter)*

WOLF: You called?

WICKED: My dear wolves, tear them to pieces! *(cackles)*

WOLF: With pleasure!

(WOLVES exit snarling; moments later, screams heard backstage; WOLF enters)

WICKED: What happened?!

WOLF: The Tin man chopped all 40 of us! Oh, the pain! *(dies)*

WICKED: Oh darn! *(whistles twice; CROWS enter)*

CROW: You called?!

WICKED: Yes crows. Peck out their eyes and tear them to pieces!

CROW: Absolutely!

(CROWS exit cawing; moments later, screams heard backstage; CROW enters)

WICKED: What now?!

CROW: The scarecrow did us in! Oh, the misery! *(dies)*

WICKED: Seriously?! Well, dag-nammit! *(blows whistle 3 times; BEES enter buzzing)*

BEE: What happened to them?

WICKED: Just ignore them, bees. They are... sleeping? Yeah.

BEE: Sleeping? *(looks at audience, concerned)* Okay...

WICKED: Go to the strangers and sting them to death!

BEE: Of course!

(BEES exit; moments later screams heard backstage; BEE enters)

BEE: NOW I know what happened to them! *(dies)*

WICKED: Bummer! Hmmm... this probably won't work, but... oh, Winkies!

(WINKIES enter, scared)

WINKIE 1: Y-y-yes...

WICKED: Go get them.

WINKIE 2: Us?!

WICKED: Y-y-yes, you! NOW GO!

(WINKIES run offstage, LION roars! WINKIES run on, across, and offstage, screaming!)

WICKED: *(to audience)* Pathetic. Am I right? Time for the winged monkeys!

(pulls out Golden Cap, says magic words; MONKEYS enter)

MONKEY: Ewww, what happened here?

WICKED: Here? Someone failing to do their job!

MONKEY: We never fail. What do you need?

WICKED: Destroy that group and bring me the lion. I'll make him work. But be careful, they've proven to be a bit *(references dead creatures)* challenging.

MONKEY: We like a challenge.

WICKED: Great. Now go!

(MONKEYS fly off, WITCH exits cackling)

ACT 2 SCENE 4

SCARECROW: Did you see how I got rid of those crows?!

TIN: And how I took care of those wolves?!

LION: And my fantastic roar!

DOROTHY: You were all so smart, caring, and brave!

TOTO: *(agrees enthusiastically)* Ruh-Ruh!

(MONKEYS heard offstage)

LION: W-w-what's that noise?

TIN: Whatever it is, I'll get them with my axe!

SCARECROW: Oh no! It's the…

ALL: WINGED MONKEYS!

(MONKEYS enter; everyone scrambles around; MONKEYS grab SCARECROW, TIN, and LION, and take them offstage separately; DOROTHY and TOTO remain center)

DOROTHY: You are awful, awful monkeys! I hope they put you in a zoo!

(MONKEYS gather around DOROTHY and growling TOTO)

MONKEY: What is this? You have a magical mark upon you.

DOROTHY: I do. Now stand back!

MONKEY: Listen monkeys, we can't kill this one, so let's bring her back to the witch.

DOROTHY: Unhand me, you flea-riddled cretins!

MONKEY: There, there, this isn't personal. Just business.

(MONKEYS take DOROTHY and TOTO offstage)

ACT 2 SCENE 5

(MONKEYS enter with LION, DOROTHY, and TOTO; WICKED enters opposite)

WICKED: Take the Lion away! And why isn't she dead?!

MONKEY: You see the mark? *(WICKED looks)* Yeah, that.

WICKED: I also see those shoes. NIIICE!!! They will go well with my shoe collection.

DOROTHY: Okay, that's it. You can shred the scarecrow, you can ruin the tin man, you can even cage the lion, but gloves are coming off if you're going to take my shoes!

WICKED: Okay, you're right. My bad. Oh, would you look at that! *(points opposite)*

DOROTHY: *(looks away)* What?

WICKED: *(grabs for shoes)* They're mine!

DOROTHY: Get away!!! *(TOTO growls)*

WICKED: Fine! Then mop these floors. NOW!

DOROTHY: You're so mean!

WICKED: Yes. Yes, I am! *(cackles)*

(DOROTHY and TOTO exit; MONKEYS exit with LION)

WICKED: *(to audience)* I'll get those shoes, yet! My closet demands it!!! And, of course, they're magical!

(DOROTHY returns with sponge and bucket, TOTO to side)

WICKED: You see this area? Mop it all!

DOROTHY: You are cruel.

WICKED: Yes, yes, yes. I've heard them all. Wicked, cruel, vicious, smelly.

DOROTHY: Smelly?

WICKED: Don't ask. Now, clean!

(DOROTHY cleans on knees downstage facing away from WICKED)

WICKED: There you go, over there a bit more.

(WICKED sneaks up behind DOROTHY, pretends to be looking at her mopping; creative fun could be had with this interchange; then finally grabs one shoe from DOROTHY'S feet)

WICKED: Ha, ha! It's mine!!

DOROTHY: What?! How dare you! *(picks up bucket and throws water at WICKED who gives loud cry of fear and begins melting away; WINKIES and LION enter)*

WICKED: See what you have done!

DOROTHY: Whoops! I'm very sorry indeed!

WICKED: Sorry?! But I'm mellltttttiiiinnnggg!

DOROTHY: Well, next time, don't touch my shoes! Ding-dong!

WICKED: Aghhhhhhhhhhhhhhhhhhhhhhhhhhhhhhhhh!!!! *(dies)*

(ALL cheer)

DOROTHY: Winkies, you are now free!

(ALL cheer)

LION: But, I am sad. Our friends are now gone.

WINKIE 1: We can help you.

WINKIE 2: Yes, we can rescue them.

WINKIE 3: We saw where the monkeys dumped them.

DOROTHY: You would help us?

WINKIES: Oh yes!

DOROTHY: Oh please, please. Thank you!

WINKIE 1: Let's go!

(WINKIES exit)

LION: Oh, I hope they find them!

(WINKIES enter with TIN and SCARECROW; ALL hug)

DOROTHY: This is so wonderful! But, we must go back to Oz, and claim his promise.

TIN: Yes! At last, I shall get my heart!

SCARECROW: And I shall get my brains.

LION: And I shall get my courage.

DOROTHY: And I shall get back to Kansas.

ALL: Yay!

TOTO: Rone?

DOROTHY: Maybe.

TOTO: Roh.

WINKIE 1: Can't the tin man stay?

WINKIE 2: Yes! He's shiny, and we want him to rule over us!

TIN: Ah, you guys are cute. But we must go back. I need my heart.

WINKIE 3: Okay, but take the Golden Cap. With it, you can call the winged monkeys!

DOROTHY: Really?!

WINKIE 1: Sure! Try it! Say the magic words inside the hat.

DOROTHY: Ok, here I go! *(says magical words; MONKEYS fly onstage)*

MONKEY: What is your command?

DOROTHY: We wish to go to the Emerald City.

MONKEY: Well, buckle up!

ALL: Bye!

(ALL exit)

ACT 3 SCENE 1

(enter DOROTHY and gang; enter GUARD opposite)

DOROTHY: We are here to see the wizard.

GUARD: Wow! You came back?

TIN: Of course, why wouldn't we?

GUARD: I just thought... ahhh... well... never mind.

SCARECROW: You thought she would kill us?

GUARD: Maybe? Or maybe do her bidding?

DOROTHY: Well, we melted her. Let Oz know we're here to collect!

GUARD: Okey-dokey! *(exits; returns moments later)* Soooo, he said he needs to think about it, and he'll see you tomorrow. And when I say tomorrow, I mean he will keep blowing you off for like a week or two.

LION: What?! Tell him we will see him NOW!

GUARD: All right, all right! Pushy... *(leads them around stage)* Here we are!

SCARECROW: Where is he?

GUARD: He's everywhere! *(motions all around)* Okay, later! *(exits)*

(OZ peeks out from behind curtain, not seen by others, but is seen by audience)

DOROTHY: Hello?

OZ: HELLO!!! I am Oz, the Great and Terrible. Why do you seek me?

DOROTHY: We did what you asked. The Wicked Witch was destroyed.

TIN: We have come to claim our promise, O Oz.

OZ: Promise? What promise?

SCARECROW: Are you kidding us?

OZ: Well, come to me tomorrow, I need to think it over.

DOROTHY: Tomorrow? Oh, no you don't.

SCARECROW: We shan't wait a day longer.

TIN: You must keep your promises!

OZ: Yessss, I just need a bit more...

LION: ROARRRRRRRR!!!!

(everyone jumps back scared, TOTO runs offstage and pulls on OZ)

DOROTHY: Who are you?

OZ: I am Oz, the great and terrible? *(TOTO growls)*

TIN: You seem more like a wazzz.

OZ: I suppose you're right. I'm just a common man.

DOROTHY: Common man? Where are you from?

OZ: I was born in Omaha.

SCARECROW: Ooh, sounds exotic.

TIN: Like a tropical beach!

LION: Or an island!

DOROTHY: Omaha!

TIN: *(to LION and SCARECROW)* I'm guessing not exotic.

DOROTHY: You are a very bad man!

OZ: Oh, no, my dear; I'm really a very good man, but I'm a very bad wizard.

DOROTHY: Okay, Mr. Omaha, how are you going to help us?

SCARECROW: Yes, I want my brains!

TIN: And my heart!

LION: And my c-c-c-courage.

TOTO: Rone?

OZ: You know, I think I can help you.

DOROTHY: And Kansas?

OZ: I should have an answer for that as well.

TIN: When can we start?

OZ: Now! Give me a moment. *(goes back stage and returns with "stuff"; DOROTHY and gang share excitement)* You realize the qualities you seek, you have possessed all along. But, as a symbolic gesture, please come sit. *(motions SCARECROW to chair)*

SCARECROW: My brains?

OZ: Your brains.

SCARECROW: I'm soooo excited!!! *(sits in chair facing audience; others watch; OZ winks at audience, pulls "brain" out of his bag)*

ALL: Oooooh.

OZ: Now sit back. *(sleight-of-hand hides "brain")* a little in here. *(places "brain" under hat)* And there you go. A head with brains!

ALL: Ahhhhhh.

DOROTHY: How do you feel?

SCARECROW: I feel wise indeed. Ask me a question!

TIN: What is the world record for the most socks put on one foot in one minute? *(or some other random fact)*

SCARECROW: 52!

(everyone cheers)

TIN: I'm next!

OZ: *(pulls out a symbolic heart)* Isn't it a beauty?

TIN: It is, indeed! But is it a kind heart?

OZ: Oh, very! I'll need to place it on your chest, is that okay?

TIN: Yes!

(OZ places heart on TIN)

OZ: There, now you have a heart any might be proud of.

TIN: Oh, thank you! Thank you!

OZ: Lion?

LION: P-p-please!

(pulls out bottle with liquid)

OZ: Drink.

LION: What is it?

OZ: Consider it... liquid courage.

LION: People drink this?

OZ: All the time. Remember, courage is always inside one. The sooner you drink, the sooner you will have your courage.

LION: Ok, bottoms up. For courage!

ALL: Courage!

(LION drinks)

OZ: How do you feel now?

LION: Full of courage! *(roars proudly)*

DOROTHY: And Kansas?

OZ: Balloon!

DOROTHY: Balloon?

OZ: Balloon.

SCARECROW: *(looks at others)* I'm the smart one, and I don't even get that.

OZ: We will fly out of here by balloon!

DOROTHY: Yay!

OZ: Mr. Brains, I leave you in charge.

SCARECROW: Yes!

OZ: My balloon is just over there, let's go!

(DOROTHY, OZ, and TOTO exit)

TIN: They didn't even say goodbye! *(starts crying)*

LION: Don't rust, Tin man!

SCARECROW: I hope Toto finally gets his bone!

(TOTO runs across stage)

TOTO: Rone?

(DOROTHY chases)

DOROTHY: Toto!

LION: Oh, you're back already! Yay!

OZ: *(from backstage)* Goodbye!

DOROTHY: Noooooooooooooooooo!!!! He left us. *(melodramatically sobs)*

LION: Oh, that's a bummer.

TIN: There, there, Dorothy. I'm sure there's another way.

DOROTHY: But I just want to go to Kansas!

SCARECROW: I know who could help us! Why not call the winged monkeys?

DOROTHY: Oh, yes!

LION: Wow, you are smart.

SCARECROW: Thank you!

(enter MONKEY)

TIN: That was fast.

MONKEY: Short play.

DOROTHY: Can you take me back to Kansas?

MONKEY: Sorry, can't cross the desert. Well, our work is done here. Later.

(MONKEYS exit)

DOROTHY: Well, that stinks!

SCARECROW: I know! Glinda the Good Witch!

(MONKEYS enter)

MONKEY: You need us again, don't you?

DOROTHY: Can you take us to Glinda the Good Witch?

MONKEY: That we can do.

(MONKEYS carry everyone offstage)

ACT 3 SCENE 2

(MONKEYS bring everyone onstage, GLINDA enters opposite)

GLINDA: Hello. What can I do for you, my child? Nice shoes by the way.

SCARECROW: Dorothy here, needs to go home.

GLINDA: I can help. But you must give me the golden cap.

DOROTHY: Willingly! *(gives cap)* It didn't really go with my outfit.

GLINDA: What will you do when Dorothy has left?

SCARECROW: I'll return to the Emerald City and be their leader.

TIN: I will go to the land of the Winkies, and rule over them.

LION: I want to be the King of the Forest.

GLINDA: Very well, the winged monkeys will take you.

LION, SCARECROW, & TIN: Thank you!

GLINDA: And my winged friends, you may keep the Golden Cap and be free for evermore.

MONKEY: Thank you. It sure was getting tiresome flying all these people around with no pay.

DOROTHY: You are certainly as good as you are beautiful! Buuuut, what about Kansas?!

GLINDA: Your silver shoes will carry you over the desert, and back home.

DOROTHY: What?! I could've gone home from the very beginning?

GLINDA: Certainly. But you wouldn't have had this wonderful adventure and helped your new friends.

DOROTHY: Well, okay, that's true! Oh, I am so going to miss you all!

(ALL hug; TIN sobbing)

SCARECROW: Be careful Tin Man, you might rust again.

TIN: I know, it's this gosh darn heart!

GLINDA: Now Dorothy, all you have to do is to knock the heels together three times and command the shoes to carry you wherever you wish to go.

DOROTHY: *(grabs TOTO, clicks heels together)* Take me home to Aunt Em! *(they start spinning and fall asleep while MONKEYS exit with LION, TIN, and SCARECROW; GLINDA exits; enter EM and HENRY running to DOROTHY'S side; DOROTHY and TOTO wake)*

EM: My darling child! Where have you been?

DOROTHY: The Land of Oz. Nice new house, by the way.

HENRY: Thanks, the other blew away in that tornado.

DOROTHY: Yeah, I know. I'm so glad to be home again! There's no place like home!

EM: Come, child. Let's get you some food and that dog a bone.

TOTO: Roooohhh!!!!

(ALL exit)

THE END

Author's note and Special Thanks

My biggest shout out goes to Isidro! He is constantly supporting me, encouraging me, and giving me snarky and witty feedback! (and he got me into The Drama Book Shop in NYC!)

Now to my Beta Readers, without you, I would make so many mistakes it's silly! So, thank you Betas!

Most specifically: Christina Robart (All About Improv), Isidro, Sandra, Royce, Rosemary, Amy, Lizette, Kevin, Lisa, Jerry, Bridget, Laura, David B., and Jennifer R.

ANNNNNNND.... The classes who workshopped this play:

Mrs. Olson's 23/24 5th Grade Literature Class and don't forget Elsie!

Mr. Rod's Foundations of Theatre 2 class-2024

David Ello's 23/24 6th Grade Drama students at Old Orchard Junior High. :-)

Cydia Sosa and the 23/24 Grant Middle School Production Class

Thank you all!

-Brendan P. Kelso
Break some legs!

ABOUT THE AUTHOR

BRENDAN P. KELSO came to writing modified Shakespeare scripts when he was taking time off from work to be at home with his newly born son. "It just grew from there". Within months, he was being asked to offer classes in various locations and acting organizations along the Central Coast of California. Originally employed as an engineer, Brendan never thought about writing. However, his unique personality, humor, and love for engaging the kids with The Bard has led him to leave the engineering world and pursue writing as a new adventure in life! He has always believed, "the best way to learn is to have fun!" Brendan makes his home on the Central Coast of California and loves to spend time with his wife and kids.

CAST AUTOGRAPHS

www.ingramcontent.com/pod-product-compliance
Lightning Source LLC
Chambersburg PA
CBHW060820050426
42449CB00008B/1747